Granny Square Stitch Guide

Get ready to mix it up! This exciting stitch guide presents 12 variations of the classic granny square, plus 10 bonus blocks that jazz up a sampler throw.

LEISURE ARTS, INC.
Maumelle, Arkansas

Library of Congress Control Number: 2015955193
ISBN-13/EAN: 978-1-4647-3882-1
UPC: 0-28906-75540-4

With more than 800 knit and crochet designs in print, Melissa Leapman is one of the most widely published American designers working today. Through the years, her patterns have appeared in dozens of nationally known magazines, while her books and classes on knitting and crochet are consistently popular with the public. Melissa has been a featured guest on numerous television shows, is a popular guest blogger, and is the host of several Leisure Arts knitting and crocheting DVDs. Nationally, her workshops are popular with crafters of all skill levels.

To find more of Melissa's exciting designs, visit LeisureArts.com, "like" Melissa's Facebook page, and join her group (Melissa Leapman Rocks) on Ravelry.com.

TABLE OF CONTENTS

1. Daisy

EASY

Finished Size: 8" (20.5 cm) square

SHOPPING LIST

Yarn (Medium Weight) MEDIUM 4

- ☐ Berry - 31 yards (28.5 meters)
- ☐ Dk Green - 22 yards (20 meters)
- ☐ Gold - 12 yards (11 meters)

Crochet Hook

- ☐ Size I (5.5 mm) **or** size need for gauge

GAUGE INFORMATION

Rnds 1-3 = 3" (7.5 cm) square

STITCH GUIDE

PUFF ST (uses one sc)

★ YO, insert hook in sc indicated, YO and pull up a loop; repeat from ★ 3 times **more**, YO and draw through all 9 loops on hook.

INSTRUCTIONS

With Gold, ch 4; join with slip st to form a ring.

Rnd 1 (Right side)**:** Ch 1, 8 sc in ring; join with slip st to first sc, finish off.

Note: Loop a short piece of yarn around any sc to mark Rnd 1 as **right** side.

Rnd 2: With **right** side facing, join Berry with slip st in any sc; work Puff St in same st, ch 3, (work Puff St in next sc, ch 3) around; join with slip st to top of first Puff St, finish off: 8 Puff Sts and 8 ch-3 sps.

Rnd 3: With **right** side facing, join Dk Green with dc in any ch-3 sp ***(see Joining With Dc, page 92)***; (dc, ch 3, 2 dc) in same sp, 4 dc in next ch-3 sp, ★ (2 dc, ch 3, 2 dc) in next ch-3 sp, 4 dc in next ch-3 sp; repeat from ★ 2 times **more**; join with slip st to first dc: 32 dc and 4 ch-3 sps.

Rnd 4: Ch 3 **(counts as first dc, now and throughout)**, dc in next dc, (2 dc, ch 3, 2 dc) in next corner ch-3 sp, ★ dc in next 8 dc, (2 dc, ch 3, 2 dc) in next corner ch-3 sp; repeat from ★ 2 times **more**, dc in last 6 dc; join with slip st to first dc: 48 dc and 4 ch-3 sps.

Rnd 5: Ch 3, dc in next 3 dc, (2 dc, ch 3, 2 dc) in next corner ch-3 sp, ★ dc in next 12 dc, (2 dc, ch 3, 2 dc) in next corner ch-3 sp; repeat from ★ 2 times **more**, dc in last 8 dc; join with slip st to first dc, finish off: 64 dc and 4 ch-3 sps.

Rnd 6: With **right** side facing, join Berry with dc in any corner ch-3 sp; (dc, ch 3, 2 dc) in same sp, dc in next 16 dc, ★ (2 dc, ch 3, 2 dc) in next corner ch-3 sp, dc in next 16 dc; repeat from ★ 2 times **more**; join with slip st to first dc: 80 dc and 4 ch-3 sps.

Rnd 7: Ch 3, dc in next dc, (2 dc, ch 3, 2 dc) in next corner ch-3 sp, ★ dc in next 20 dc, (2 dc, ch 3, 2 dc) in next corner ch-3 sp; repeat from ★ 2 times **more**, dc in last 18 dc; join with slip st to first dc, finish off: 96 dc and 4 ch-3 sps.

Rnd 8: With **right** side facing, join Gold with sc in any corner ch-3 sp ***(see Joining With Sc, page 92)***; 2 sc in same sp, (sc in each dc across to next corner ch-3 sp, 5 sc in corner ch-3 sp) 3 times, sc in each dc across, 2 sc in same sp as first sc; join with slip st to first sc, finish off leaving a long end for sewing: 116 sc.

2. Concentric Circles

EASY

Finished Size: 8" (20.5 cm) sqaure

SHOPPING LIST

Yarn (Medium Weight) MEDIUM 4

- ☐ Dk Green - 46 yards (42 meters)
- ☐ Gold - 15 yards (13.5 meters)

Crochet Hook

- ☐ Size I (5.5 mm) **or** size need for gauge

GAUGE INFORMATION

Rnds 1 and 2 = 3¼" (8.25 cm) diameter

STITCH GUIDE

TREBLE CROCHET *(abbreviated tr)*

YO twice, insert hook in sc indicated, YO and pull up a loop (4 loops on hook), (YO and draw through 2 loops on hook) 3 times.

INSTRUCTIONS

With Dk Green, ch 4; join with slip st to form a ring.

Rnd 1 (Right side)**:** Ch 3 **(counts as first dc, now and throughout)**, 15 dc in ring; join with slip st to first dc, finish off: 16 dc.

Note: Loop a short piece of yarn around any dc to mark Rnd 1 as **right** side.

Rnd 2: With **right** side facing, join Gold with dc in any dc *(see Joining With Dc, page 92)*; dc in same st, 2 dc in next dc and in each dc around; join with slip st to first dc, finish off: 32 dc.

Rnd 3: With **right** side facing, join Dk Green with dc in any dc; dc in same st and in next dc, (2 dc in next dc, dc in next dc) around; join with slip st to first dc, finish off: 48 dc.

Rnd 4: With **right** side facing, join Gold with dc in any dc; dc in same st and in next 2 dc, (2 dc in next dc, dc in next 2 dc) around; join with slip st to first dc, finish off: 64 dc.

Rnd 5: With **right** side facing, join Dk Green with sc in any dc *(see Joining With Sc, page 92)*; (ch 5, skip next 3 dc, sc in next dc) around to last 3 dc, ch 2, skip last 3 dc, dc in first sc to form last ch-5 sp; do **not** finish off: 16 sc and 16 ch-5 sps.

Rnd 6: Ch 1, 3 sc in last ch-5 sp made, 5 sc in next ch-5 sp and in each ch-5 sp around, 2 sc in same sp as first sc; join with slip st to first sc: 80 sc.

Rnd 7: Ch 4 **(counts as first tr)**, ★ † tr in next 2 sc, dc in next 2 sc, hdc in next 2 sc, sc in next 7 sc, hdc in next 2 sc, dc in next 2 sc, tr in next 2 sc †, (tr, ch 3, tr) in next sc; repeat from ★ 2 times **more**, then repeat from † to † once, tr in same st as first tr, ch 1, hdc in first tr to form last ch-3 sp: 84 sts and 4 ch-3 sps.

Rnd 8: Ch 3, dc in last ch-3 sp made and in next 21 sts, ★ (2 dc, ch 2, 2 dc) in next corner ch-3 sp, dc in next 21 sts; repeat from ★ 2 times **more**, 2 dc in same sp as first dc, ch 1, sc in first dc to form last ch-2 sp; finish off leaving a long end for sewing: 100 dc and 4 ch-2 sps.

3. Zinnia

EASY +

Finished Size: 8" (20.5 cm) square

SHOPPING LIST

Yarn (Medium Weight) 4 MEDIUM

- ☐ Berry - 23 yards (21 meters)
- ☐ Gold - 23 yards (21 meters)
- ☐ Rust - 11 yards (10 meters)

Crochet Hook

- ☐ Size I (5.5 mm)
  or size need for gauge

GAUGE INFORMATION

Rnds 1 and 2 = 2¼" (5.75 cm) diameter

INSTRUCTIONS

With Berry, ch 5; join with slip st to form a ring.

Rnd 1 (Right side)**:** Ch 1, 12 sc in ring; join with slip st to first sc.

Note: Loop a short piece of yarn around any sc to mark Rnd 1 as **right** side.

Rnd 2: Ch 3 (**counts as first dc, now and throughout**), dc in same sc as joining, 2 dc in next sc and in each sc around; join with slip st to first dc: 24 dc.

Rnd 3: Ch 1, sc in same dc as joining and in next dc, ch 7, (sc in next 2 sc, ch 7) around; join with slip st to first sc, finish off: 24 sc and 12 ch-7 sps.

Rnd 4: With **right** side facing, join Gold with sc in any ch-7 sp ***(see Joining With Sc, page 92)***; 2 sc in same sp, 3 sc in each of next 2 ch-7 sps, ch 5, (3 sc in each of next 3 ch-7 sps, ch 5) 3 times; join with slip st to first sc: 36 sc and 4 ch-5 sps.

Rnd 5: Ch 3, dc in next 8 sc, (3 dc, ch 3, 3 dc) in next corner ch-5 sp, ★ dc in next 9 sc, (3 dc, ch 3, 3 dc) in next corner ch-5 sp; repeat from ★ 2 times **more**; join with slip st to first dc, finish off: 60 dc and 4 ch-3 sps.

Rnd 6: With **right** side facing, join Rust with dc in any corner ch-3 sp *(see Joining With Dc, page 92)*; (dc, ch 3, 2 dc) in same sp, ★ dc in each dc across to next corner ch-3 sp, (2 dc, ch 3, 2 dc) in corner ch-3 sp; repeat from ★ 2 times **more**, dc in each dc across; join with slip st to first dc, finish off: 76 dc and 4 ch-3 sps.

Rnd 7: With **right** side facing, join Berry with dc in any corner ch-3 sp; (dc, ch 3, 2 dc) in same sp, ★ dc in each dc across to next corner ch-3 sp, (2 dc, ch 3, 2 dc) in corner ch-3 sp; repeat from ★ 2 times **more**, dc in each dc across; join with slip st to first dc, finish off: 92 dc and 4 ch-3 sps.

Rnd 8: With **right** side facing, join Gold with sc in any corner ch-3 sp; sc in same sp, ★ sc in each dc across to next corner ch-3 sp, 3 sc in corner ch-3 sp; repeat from ★ 2 times **more**, sc in each dc across and in same sp as first sc; join with slip st to first sc, finish off leaving a long end for sewing: 104 sc.

4. Garden Flower

EASY +

Finished Size: 8" (20.5 cm) square

SHOPPING LIST

Yarn (Medium Weight) MEDIUM 4

- ☐ Lt Green - 49 yards (45 meters)
- ☐ Rust - 19 yards (17.5 meters)
- ☐ Gold - 13 yards (12 meters)

Crochet Hook

- ☐ Size I (5.5 mm) **or** size need for gauge

GAUGE INFORMATION

Rnd 1 = 1¾" (4.5 cm) diameter

Rnds 1-7 = 4½" (11.5 cm) square

INSTRUCTIONS

With Gold, ch 5; join with slip st to form a ring.

Rnd 1 (Right side)**:** Ch 3 **(counts as first dc, now and throughout)**, 17 dc in ring; join with slip st to first dc: 18 dc.

Note: Loop a short piece of yarn around any dc to mark Rnd 1 as **right** side.

Rnd 2: Ch 1, sc in same st, ch 3, skip next 2 dc, ★ sc in next dc, ch 3, skip next 2 dc; repeat from ★ around; join with slip st to first sc: 6 ch-3 sps.

Rnd 3: Ch 1, (sc, ch 3, 6 dc, ch 3, sc) in each ch-3 sp around; join with slip st to first sc, finish off: 6 petals.

Rnd 4: With **right** side facing, join Rust with sc in first sc on any petal *(see Joining With Sc, page 92)*; ch 5, ★ keeping ch **behind** petal, sc in first sc on next petal, ch 5; repeat from ★ around; keeping ch **behind** petal, join with slip st to first sc: 6 ch-5 sps.

Rnd 5: Ch 1, (sc, ch 3, 8 dc, ch 3, sc) in each ch-5 sp around; join with slip st to first sc, finish off: 6 petals.

Rnd 6: With **right** side facing, join Lt Green with sc in first sc on any petal; ch 6, ★ keeping ch **behind** petal, sc in first sc on next petal, ch 6; repeat from ★ around; keeping ch **behind** petal, join with slip st to first sc: 6 ch-6 sps.

Rnd 7: Slip st in first ch-6 sp, ch 3, (4 dc, ch 2, dc) in same sp, 6 dc in next ch-6 sp, (2 dc, ch 2, 4 dc) in next ch-6 sp, (5 dc, ch 2, dc) in next ch-6 sp, 6 dc in next ch-6 sp, (2 dc, ch 2, 4 dc) in last ch-6 sp; join with slip st to first dc: 36 dc and 4 ch-2 sps.

Rnd 8: Ch 3, dc in next 4 dc, (3 dc, ch 2, 3 dc) in next corner ch-2 sp, ★ dc in next 9 dc, (3 dc, ch 2, 3 dc) in next corner ch-2 sp; repeat from ★ 2 times **more**, dc in last 4 dc; join with slip st to first dc: 60 dc and 4 ch-2 sps.

Rnd 9: Ch 3, dc in next 7 dc, (3 dc, ch 2, 3 dc) in next corner ch-2 sp, ★ dc in next 15 dc, (3 dc, ch 2, 3 dc) in next corner ch-2 sp; repeat from ★ 2 times **more**, dc in last 7 dc; join with slip st to first dc, finish off: 84 dc and 4 ch-2 sps.

Rnd 10: With **right** side facing, join Rust with sc in any corner ch-2 sp; ch 1, sc in same sp, ch 1, skip next dc, (sc in next dc, ch 1, skip next dc) 10 times, ★ (sc, ch 1) twice in next corner ch-2 sp, skip next dc, (sc in next dc, ch 1, skip next dc) 10 times; repeat from ★ 2 times **more**; join with slip st to first sc, finish off: 48 sc and 48 ch-1 sps.

Rnd 11: With **right** side facing, join Lt Green with sc in any corner ch-1 sp; sc in same sp and in next sc, (sc in next ch-1 sp and in next sc) 11 times, ★ 3 sc in next corner ch-1 sp, sc in next sc, (sc in next ch-1 sp and in next sc) 11 times; repeat from ★ 2 times **more**, sc in same sp as first sc; join with slip st to first sc: 104 sc.

Rnd 12: Ch 1, 2 sc in same st, ★ sc in each sc across to center sc of next corner 3-sc group, 3 sc in center sc; repeat from ★ 2 times **more**, sc in each sc across and in same st as first sc; join with slip st to first sc, finish off leaving a long end for sewing: 112 sc.

5. Zesty Popcorns

EASY +

Finished Size: 8" (20.5 cm) square

SHOPPING LIST

Yarn (Medium Weight) MEDIUM 4

- ☐ Rust - 35 yards (32 meters)
- ☐ Berry - 30 yards (27.5 meters)
- ☐ Lt Green - 18 yards (16.5 meters)

Crochet Hook

- ☐ Size I (5.5 mm) **or** size need for gauge

GAUGE INFORMATION

Rnds 1 and 2 = 2½" (6.25 cm) square

STITCH GUIDE

BEGINNING POPCORN

Ch 3, 4 dc in ring, drop loop from hook, insert hook in top of beginning ch 3, hook dropped loop and draw through st.

POPCORN (uses one st or sp)

5 Dc in st or sp indicated, drop loop from hook, insert hook in first dc of 5-dc group, hook dropped loop and draw through st.

INSTRUCTIONS

With Rust, ch 4; join with slip st to form a ring.

Rnd 1 (Right side)**:** Work Beginning Popcorn, ch 3, (work Popcorn in ring, ch 3) 3 times; join with slip st to top of Beginning Popcorn, finish off: 4 Popcorns and 4 ch-3 sps.

Note: Loop a short piece of yarn around any stitch to mark Rnd 1 as **right** side.

Rnd 2: With **right** side facing, join Berry with dc in same st as joining ***(see Joining With Dc, page 92)***; (2 dc, ch 3, 2 dc) in next ch-3 sp, ★ dc in next Popcorn, (2 dc, ch 3, 2 dc) in next ch-3 sp; repeat from ★ 2 times **more**; join with slip st to first dc: 20 dc and 4 ch-3 sps.

Rnd 3: Ch 3 **(counts as first dc, now and throughout)**, dc in next 2 dc, (2 dc, ch 3, 2 dc) in next corner ch-3 sp, ★ dc in next 5 dc, (2 dc, ch 3, 2 dc) in next corner ch-3 sp; repeat from ★ 2 times **more**, dc in last 2 dc; join with slip st to first dc, finish off: 36 dc and 4 ch-3 sps.

Rnd 4: With **right** side facing, join Lt Green with dc in same dc as joining; (work Popcorn in next dc, dc in next dc) twice, work (Popcorn, ch 3, Popcorn) in next corner ch-3 sp, ★ dc in next dc, (work Popcorn in next dc, dc in next dc) 4 times, work (Popcorn, ch 3, Popcorn) in next corner ch-3 sp; repeat from ★ 2 times **more**, (dc in next dc, work Popcorn in next dc) twice; join with slip st to first dc, finish off: 20 dc, 24 Popcorns, and 4 ch-3 sps.

Rnd 5: With **right** side facing, join Berry with dc in same dc as joining; dc in next Popcorn, (dc in next dc and in next Popcorn) twice, (2 dc, ch 3, 2 dc) in next corner ch-3 sp, ★ dc in next Popcorn, (dc in next dc and in next Popcorn) 5 times, (2 dc, ch 3, 2 dc) in next corner ch-3 sp; repeat from ★ 2 times **more**, dc in next Popcorn, (dc in next dc and in next Popcorn) twice; join with slip st to first dc: 60 dc and 4 ch-3 sps.

Rnd 6: Ch 3, dc in next 7 dc, (2 dc, ch 3, 2 dc) in next corner ch-3 sp, ★ dc in next 15 dc, (2 dc, ch 3, 2 dc) in next corner ch-3 sp; repeat from ★ 2 times **more**, dc in last 7 dc; join with slip st to first dc, finish off: 76 dc and 4 ch-3 sps.

Rnd 7: With **right** side facing, join Rust with dc in first dc **after** any corner ch-3 sp; (work Popcorn in next dc, dc in next dc) 9 times, work (Popcorn, ch 3, Popcorn) in next corner ch-3 sp, ★ dc in next dc, (work Popcorn in next dc, dc in next dc) 9 times, work (Popcorn, ch 3, Popcorn) in next corner ch-3 sp; repeat from ★ 2 times **more**; join with slip st to first dc, finish off: 40 dc, 44 Popcorns, and 4 ch-3 sps.

Rnd 8: With **right** side facing, join Berry with sc in any corner ch-3 sp ***(see Joining With Sc, page 92)***; sc in same sp, ★ sc in each Popcorn and in each dc across to next corner ch-3 sp, 3 sc in corner ch-3 sp; repeat from ★ 2 times **more**, sc in each Popcorn and in each dc across, sc in same sp as first sc; join with slip st to first sc, finish off leaving a long end for sewing: 96 sc.

6. Chrysanthemum

EASY

Finished Size: 8" (20.5 cm) square

SHOPPING LIST

Yarn (Medium Weight) MEDIUM 4

- ☐ Rust - 27 yards (24.5 meters)
- ☐ Purple - 18 yards (16.5 meters)

Crochet Hook

- ☐ Size I (5.5 mm) **or** size need for gauge

GAUGE INFORMATION

Rnds 1 and 2 = 2½" (6.25 cm) diameter

INSTRUCTIONS

With Purple, ch 6; join with slip st to form a ring.

Rnd 1 (Right side)**:** Ch 1, ★ sc in ring, ch 12, (sc in ring, ch 8) twice; repeat from ★ 3 times **more**; join with slip st to first sc, finish off: 4 loops and 8 ch-8 sps.

Note: Loop a short piece of yarn around any sc to mark Rnd 1 as **right** side.

Rnd 2: With **right** side facing, join Rust with dc in any loop ***(see Joining With Dc, page 92)***; (dc, ch 2, 2 dc) in same sp, 2 sc in each of next 2 ch-8 sps, ★ (2 dc, ch 2, 2 dc) in next loop, 2 sc in each of next 2 ch-8 sps; repeat from ★ 2 times **more**; join with slip st to first dc: 16 dc, 16 sc, and 4 ch-2 sps.

Rnd 3: Ch 3 **(counts as first dc, now and throughout)**, dc in next dc, (2 dc, ch 2, 2 dc) in next corner ch-2 sp, ★ dc in next 8 sts, (2 dc, ch 2, 2 dc) in next corner ch-2 sp; repeat from ★ 2 times **more**, dc in last 6 sts; join with slip st to first dc, finish off: 48 dc and 4 ch-2 sps.

Rnd 4: With **right** side facing, join Purple with dc in any corner ch-2 sp; (dc, ch 2, 2 dc) in same sp, dc in next 12 dc, ★ (2 dc, ch 2, 2 dc) in next corner ch-2 sp, dc in next 12 dc; repeat from ★ 2 times **more**; join with slip st to first dc, finish off: 64 dc and 4 ch-2 sps.

Rnd 5: With **right** side facing, join Rust with dc in any corner ch-2 sp; (dc, ch 2, 2 dc) in same sp, dc in next 16 dc, ★ (2 dc, ch 2, 2 dc) in next corner ch-2 sp, dc in next 16 dc; repeat from ★ 2 times **more**; join with slip st to first dc: 80 dc and 4 ch-2 sps.

Rnd 6: Ch 3, dc in next dc, (2 dc, ch 2, 2 dc) in next corner ch-2 sp, ★ dc in next 20 dc, (2 dc, ch 2, 2 dc) in next corner ch-2 sp; repeat from ★ 2 times **more**, dc in last 18 dc; join with slip st to first dc, finish off: 96 dc and 4 ch-2 sps.

Rnd 7: With **right** side facing, join Purple with sc in any corner ch-2 sp ***(see Joining With Sc, page 92)***; 2 sc in same sp, (sc in each dc across to next corner ch-2 sp, 5 sc in corner ch-2 sp) 3 times, sc in each dc across, 2 sc in same sp as first sc; join with slip st to first sc, finish off leaving a long end for sewing: 116 sc.

7. Circles in the Square

EASY +

Finished Size: 8" (20.5 cm) square

SHOPPING LIST

Yarn (Medium Weight) MEDIUM 4

- ☐ Blue - 45 yards (41 meters)
- ☐ Lt Blue - 36 yards (33 meters)

Crochet Hook

- ☐ Size I (5.5 mm) **or** size need for gauge

Additional Supplies

- ☐ Yarn needle

GAUGE INFORMATION

One Motif = 3" (7.5 cm) square

INSTRUCTIONS

Motif (Make 4)

With Lt Blue, ch 5; join with slip st to form a ring.

Rnd 1 (Right side)**:** Ch 1, 10 sc in ring; join with slip st to first sc.

Note: Loop a short piece of yarn around any sc to mark Rnd 1 as **right** side.

Rnd 2: Ch 1, sc in same st, 2 sc in next sc, (sc in next sc, 2 sc in next sc) around; join with slip st to first sc: 15 sc.

Rnd 3: Ch 1, sc in same st and in next sc, 2 sc in next sc, (sc in next 2 sc, 2 sc in next sc) around; join with slip st to first sc, finish off: 20 sc.

Rnd 4: With **right** side facing, join Blue with slip st in same st as joining; ch 5 **(counts as first dc plus ch 2)**, 2 dc in same st, sc in next 4 sc, ★ (2 dc, ch 2, 2 dc) in next sc, sc in next 4 sc; repeat from ★ 2 times **more**, dc in same st as first dc; join with slip st to first dc: 32 sts and 4 ch-2 sps.

Rnd 5: (Slip st, ch 1, 3 sc) in next corner ch-2 sp, sc in next 8 sts, (5 sc in next corner ch-2 sp, sc in next 8 sts) 3 times, 2 sc in same sp as first sc; join with slip st to first sc, finish off leaving a long end for sewing: 52 sc.

Join 2 Motifs together as follows: Thread yarn needle with long end. With **wrong** sides together, beginning in center sc of corner 5-sc group and working through **inside** loops on **both** pieces, whipstitch Motifs together ending in center sc of next corner 5-sc group ***(Fig. A)***.

Fig. A

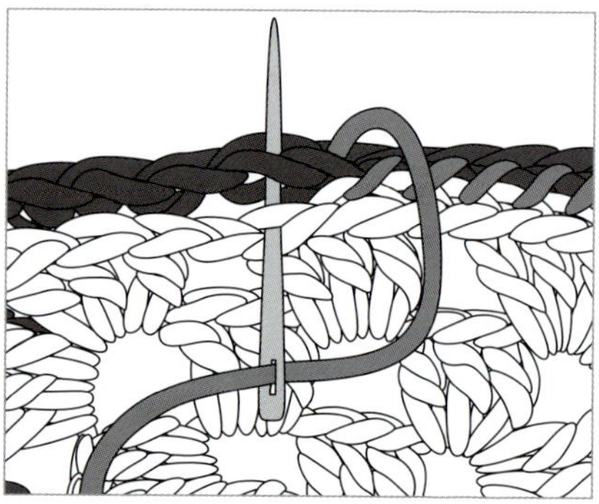

Whipstitch remaining 2 Motifs together; then whipstitch **both** pieces together to form a square.

Border

Rnd 1: With **right** side facing, join Blue with sc in center sc of any corner 5-sc group *(see Joining With Sc, page 92)*; sc in same st, ★ sc in next 12 sc, 2 sc in joining, sc in next 12 sc, 3 sc in next corner sc; repeat from ★ 2 times **more**, sc in next 12 sc, 2 sc in joining, sc in last 12 sc and in same st as first sc; join with slip st to first sc, finish off: 116 sc.

Rnd 2: With **right** side facing, join Lt Blue with sc in center sc of any corner 3-sc group; sc in same st, ★ sc in each sc across to center sc of next corner 3-sc group, 3 sc in center sc; repeat from ★ 2 times **more**, sc in each sc across and in same st as first sc; join with slip st to first sc: 124 sc.

Rnd 3: Ch 1, 2 sc in same st, ★ sc in each sc across to center sc of next corner 3-sc group, 3 sc in center sc; repeat from ★ 2 times **more**, sc in each sc across and in same st as first sc; join with slip st to first sc, finish off leaving a long end for sewing: 132 sc.

8. Ruffled

EASY +

Finished Size: 8" (20.5 cm) square

SHOPPING LIST

Yarn (Medium Weight) MEDIUM 4

- ☐ Green - 68 yards (62 meters)
- ☐ Purple - 41 yards (37.5 meters)

Crochet Hook

- ☐ Size I (5.5 mm) **or** size need for gauge

GAUGE INFORMATION

Rnds 1-3 = 3½" (9 cm) square

INSTRUCTIONS

Body

With Purple, ch 5; join with slip st to form a ring.

Rnd 1 (Right side)**:** Ch 3 **(counts as first dc, now and throughout)**, 2 dc in ring, ch 3, (3 dc in ring, ch 3) 3 times; join with slip st to first dc: 12 dc and 4 ch-3 sps.

Note: Loop a short piece of yarn around any dc to mark Rnd 1 as **right** side.

Rnd 2: Ch 4 **(counts as first dc plus ch 1, now and throughout)**, skip next dc, dc in next dc, ch 1, (dc, ch 3, dc) in next corner ch-3 sp, ch 1, ★ dc in next dc, ch 1, skip next dc, dc in next dc, ch 1, (dc, ch 3, dc) in next corner ch-3 sp, ch 1; repeat from ★ 2 times **more**; join with slip st to first dc: 16 dc and 16 sps.

Rnd 3: Ch 3, (dc in next ch-1 sp and in next dc) twice, (2 dc, ch 3, 2 dc) in next corner ch-3 sp, ★ dc in next dc, (dc in next ch-1 sp and in next dc) 3 times, (2 dc, ch 3, 2 dc) in next corner ch-3 sp; repeat from ★ 2 times **more**, dc in next dc and in last ch-1 sp; join with slip st to first dc: 44 dc and 4 ch-3 sps.

Rnd 4: Ch 4, (skip next dc, dc in next dc, ch 1) 3 times, (dc, ch 3, dc) in next corner ch-3 sp, ch 1, ★ dc in next dc, ch 1, (skip next dc, dc in next dc, ch 1) 5 times, (dc, ch 3, dc) in next corner ch-3 sp, ch 1; repeat from ★ 2 times **more**, (dc in next dc, ch 1, skip next dc) twice; join with slip st to first dc: 32 dc and 32 sps.

Rnd 5: Ch 3, (dc in next ch-1 sp and in next dc) 4 times, (2 dc, ch 3, 2 dc) in next corner ch-3 sp, ★ dc in next dc, (dc in next ch-1 sp and in next dc) 7 times, (2 dc, ch 3, 2 dc) in next corner ch-3 sp; repeat from ★ 2 times **more**, (dc in next dc and in next ch-1 sp) 3 times; join with slip st to first dc: 76 dc and 4 ch-3 sps.

Rnd 6: Ch 4, (skip next dc, dc in next dc, ch 1) 5 times, (dc, ch 3, dc) in next corner ch-3 sp, ch 1, ★ dc in next dc, ch 1, (skip next dc, dc in next dc, ch 1) 9 times, (dc, ch 3, dc) in next corner ch-3 sp, ch 1; repeat from ★ 2 times **more**, (dc in next dc, ch 1, skip next dc) 4 times; join with slip st to first dc: 48 dc and 48 sps.

Rnd 7: Ch 3, (dc in next ch-1 sp and in next dc) 6 times, (2 dc, ch 3, 2 dc) in next corner ch-3 sp, ★ dc in next dc, (dc in next ch-1 sp and in next dc) 11 times, (2 dc, ch 3, 2 dc) in next corner ch-3 sp; repeat from ★ 2 times **more**, (dc in next dc and in next ch-1 sp) 5 times; join with slip st to first dc, finish off: 108 dc and 4 ch-3 sps.

Edging Rnd: With **right** side facing, join Green with sc in any corner ch-3 sp ***(see Joining With Sc, page 92)***; sc in same sp and in each dc across to next corner ch-3 sp, 3 sc in corner ch-3 sp, ★ sc in each dc across to next corner ch-3 sp, 3 sc in corner ch-3 sp; repeat from ★ once **more**, sc in each dc across and in same sp as first sc; join with slip st to first sc, finish off leaving a long end for sewing: 120 sc.

Ruffle

With **right** side facing, join Green with slip st around any dc on Rnd 2; ch 4, (dc around same st, ch 1) twice, (dc, ch 1) 3 times around next dc and around each dc on Rnd 2; join with slip st to first dc, finish off.

Repeat Ruffle, working around dc on Rnd 4 and Rnd 6.

9. "X" Marks the Spot

EASY +

Finished Size: 8" (20.5 cm) square

SHOPPING LIST

Yarn (Medium Weight) MEDIUM 4

- ☐ Brick Red - 53 yards (48.5 meters)
- ☐ Green - 22 yards (20 meters)

Crochet Hook

- ☐ Size I (5.5 mm) **or** size need for gauge

GAUGE INFORMATION

Rnds 1-5 = 3¼" (8.25 cm) square

INSTRUCTIONS

With Green, ch 5; join with slip st to form a ring.

Rnd 1 (Right side)**:** Ch 1, 8 sc in ring; join with slip st to first sc changing to Brick Red ***(Figs. 2a & b, page 93)***, do **not** cut Green.

Note: Loop a short piece of yarn around any sc to mark Rnd 1 as **right** side.

Change color in same manner throughout, working over unused color *(Fig. 2c, page 93)*.

Rnd 2: With Brick Red ch 1, sc in same st, with Green 3 sc in next sc, (with Brick Red sc in next sc, with Green 3 sc in next sc) 3 times; join with slip st to first sc changing to Brick Red: 16 sc.

Rnd 3: With Brick Red ch 1, sc in same st and in next sc, with Green 3 sc in next sc, (with Brick Red sc in next 3 sc, with Green 3 sc in next sc) 3 times, with Brick Red sc in last sc; join with slip st to first sc: 24 sc.

Rnd 4: With Brick Red ch 1, sc in same st and in next 2 sc, with Green 3 sc in next sc, (with Brick Red sc in next 5 sc, with Green 3 sc in next sc) 3 times, with Brick Red sc in last 2 sc; join with slip st to first sc: 32 sc.

Rnd 5: With Brick Red ch 1, sc in same st and in next 3 sc, with Green 3 sc in next sc, (with Brick Red sc in next 7 sc, with Green 3 sc in next sc) 3 times, with Brick Red sc in last 3 sc; join with slip st to first sc: 40 sc.

Rnd 6: With Brick Red ch 1, sc in same st and in next 4 sc, with Green 3 sc in next sc, (with Brick Red sc in next 9 sc, with Green 3 sc in next sc) 3 times, with Brick Red sc in last 4 sc; join with slip st to first sc: 48 sc.

Rnd 7: With Brick Red ch 1, sc in same st and in next 5 sc, with Green 3 sc in next sc, (with Brick Red sc in next 11 sc, with Green 3 sc in next sc) 3 times, with Brick Red sc in last 5 sc; join with slip st to first sc: 56 sc.

Rnd 8: With Brick Red ch 1, sc in same st and in next 6 sc, with Green 3 sc in next sc, (with Brick Red sc in next 13 sc, with Green 3 sc in next sc) 3 times, with Brick Red sc in last 6 sc; join with slip st to first sc: 64 sc.

Rnd 9: With Brick Red ch 1, sc in same st and in next 7 sc, with Green 3 sc in next sc, (with Brick Red sc in next 15 sc, with Green 3 sc in next sc) 3 times, with Brick Red sc in last 7 sc; join with slip st to first sc: 72 sc.

Rnd 10: With Brick Red ch 1, sc in same st and in next 8 sc, with Green 3 sc in next sc, (with Brick Red sc in next 17 sc, with Green 3 sc in next sc) 3 times, with Brick Red sc in last 8 sc; join with slip st to first sc: 80 sc.

Rnd 11: With Brick Red ch 1, sc in same st and in next 9 sc, with Green 3 sc in next sc, (with Brick Red sc in next 19 sc, with Green 3 sc in next sc) 3 times, with Brick Red sc in last 9 sc; join with slip st to first sc: 88 sc.

Rnd 12: With Brick Red ch 1, sc in same st and in next 10 sc, with Green 3 sc in next sc, (with Brick Red sc in next 21 sc, with Green 3 sc in next sc) 3 times, with Brick Red sc in last 10 sc; join with slip st to first sc: 96 sc.

Rnd 13: With Brick Red ch 1, sc in same st and in next 11 sc, with Green 3 sc in next sc, (with Brick Red sc in next 23 sc, with Green 3 sc in next sc) 3 times, cut Green, with Brick Red sc in last 11 sc; join with slip st to first sc, finish off: 104 sc.

10. Bright Wheel

EASY

Finished Size: 8" (20.5 cm) square

SHOPPING LIST

Yarn (Medium Weight) MEDIUM 4

- ☐ Brick Red - 38 yards (34.5 meters)
- ☐ Purple - 29 yards (26.5 meters)
- ☐ Lt Blue - 6 yards (5.5 meters)

Crochet Hook

- ☐ Size I (5.5 mm) **or** size need for gauge

INSTRUCTIONS

With Brick Red, ch 5; join with slip st to form a ring.

Rnd 1 (Right side)**:** Ch 1, 12 sc in ring; join with slip st to first sc.

Note: Loop a short piece of yarn around any sc to mark Rnd 1 as **right** side.

GAUGE INFORMATION

Rnds 1-3 = 2¾" (7 cm) diameter

Rnd 2: Ch 3 (**counts as first dc, now and throughout**), dc in same st, 2 dc in next sc and in each sc around; join with slip st to first dc, finish off: 24 dc.

Rnd 3: With **right** side facing, join Purple with sc in same st as joining *(see Joining With Sc, page 92)*; ch 2, skip next dc, ★ sc in next dc, ch 2, skip next dc; repeat from ★ around; join with slip st to first sc, finish off: 12 sc and 12 ch-2 sps.

Rnd 4: With **right** side facing, join Lt Blue with dc in any ch-2 sp *(see Joining With Dc, page 92)*; dc in same sp, 3 dc in next ch-2 sp and in each ch-2 sp around, dc in same sp as first dc; join with slip st to first dc, finish off: 36 dc.

Rnd 5: With **right** side facing, join Purple with dc in same st as joining; dc in same st, hdc in next 2 dc, sc in next 4 dc, hdc in next 2 dc, ★ (2 dc, ch 2, 2 dc) in next dc, hdc in next 2 dc, sc in next 4 dc, hdc in next 2 dc; repeat from ★ 2 times **more**, 2 dc in same st as first dc, ch 1, sc in first dc to form last ch-2 sp: 48 sts and 4 ch-2 sps.

Rnd 6: Ch 3, dc in last ch-2 sp made, ★ dc in next st and in each st across to next corner ch-2 sp, (2 dc, ch 2, 2 dc) in corner ch-2 sp; repeat from ★ 2 times **more**, dc in next st and in each st across, 2 dc in same sp as first dc, ch 1, sc in first dc to form last ch-2 sp: 64 dc and 4 ch-2 sps.

Rnd 7: Ch 3, dc in last ch-2 sp made, ★ dc in next dc and in each dc across to next corner ch-2 sp, (2 dc, ch 2, 2 dc) in corner ch-2 sp; repeat from ★ 2 times **more**, dc in next dc and in each dc across, 2 dc in same sp as first dc, ch 2; join with slip st to first dc, finish off: 80 dc and 4 ch-2 sps.

Rnd 8: With **right** side facing, join Brick Red with dc in any corner ch-2 sp; dc in same sp, ★ dc in next dc and in each dc across to next corner ch-2 sp, (2 dc, ch 2, 2 dc) in corner ch-2 sp; repeat from ★ 2 times **more**, dc in next dc and in each dc across, 2 dc in same sp as first dc, ch 1, sc in first dc to form last ch-2 sp: 96 dc and 4 ch-2 sps.

Rnd 9: Ch 3, dc in last ch-2 sp made, ★ dc in next dc and in each dc across to next corner ch-2 sp, (2 dc, ch 2, 2 dc) in corner ch-2 sp; repeat from ★ 2 times **more**, dc in next dc and in each dc across, 2 dc in same sp as first dc, ch 2; join with slip st to first dc, finish off leaving a long end for sewing: 112 dc and 4 ch-2 sps.

11. Multicolored

EASY +

Finished Size: 8" (20.5 cm) square

SHOPPING LIST

Yarn (Medium Weight)

MEDIUM 4

- ☐ Brick Red - 31 yards (28.5 meters)
- ☐ Green - 24 yards (22 meters)
- ☐ Purple - 21 yards (19 meters)

Crochet Hook

- ☐ Size I (5.5 mm) **or** size need for gauge

GAUGE INFORMATION

Rnds 1 and 2 = 2¾" (7 cm) square

INSTRUCTIONS

With Brick Red, ch 5; join with slip st to form a ring.

Rnd 1 (Right side)**:** Ch 3 **(counts as first dc, now and throughout)**, 2 dc in ring, ch 2, (3 dc in ring, ch 2) 3 times; join with slip st to first dc, finish off: 12 dc and 4 ch-2 sps.

Note: Loop a short piece of yarn around any dc to mark Rnd 1 as **right** side.

Rnd 2: With **right** side facing, join Green with dc in any corner ch-2 sp *(see Joining With Dc, page 92)*; (dc, ch 2, 2 dc) in same sp, dc in next 3 dc, ★ (2 dc, ch 2, 2 dc) in next corner ch-2 sp, dc in next 3 dc; repeat from ★ 2 times **more**; join with slip st to first dc, finish off: 28 dc and 4 ch-2 sps.

Rnd 3: With **right** side facing, join Purple with dc in any corner ch-2 sp; (dc, ch 2, 2 dc) in same sp, dc in next 7 dc, ★ (2 dc, ch 2, 2 dc) in next corner ch-2 sp, dc in next 7 dc; repeat from ★ 2 times **more**; join with slip st to first dc, finish off: 44 dc and 4 ch-2 sps.

Rnd 4: With **right** side facing, join Brick Red with dc in any corner ch-2 sp; (dc, ch 2, 2 dc) in same sp, dc in next 11 dc, ★ (2 dc, ch 2, 2 dc) in next corner ch-2 sp, dc in next 11 dc; repeat from ★ 2 times **more**; join with slip st to first dc, finish off: 60 dc and 4 ch-2 sps.

Rnd 5: With **right** side facing, join Green with dc in any corner ch-2 sp; (dc, ch 2, 2 dc) in same sp, dc in next 15 dc, ★ (2 dc, ch 2, 2 dc) in next corner ch-2 sp, dc in next 15 dc; repeat from ★ 2 times **more**; join with slip st to first dc, finish off: 76 dc and 4 ch-2 sps.

Rnd 6: With **right** side facing, join Purple with dc in any corner ch-2 sp; (dc, ch 2, 2 dc) in same sp, dc in next 19 dc, ★ (2 dc, ch 2, 2 dc) in next corner ch-2 sp, dc in next 19 dc; repeat from ★ 2 times **more**; join with slip st to first dc, finish off: 92 dc and 4 ch-2 sps.

Rnd 7: With **right** side facing, join Brick Red with dc in any corner ch-2 sp; ch 2, 2 dc in same sp, dc in next 23 dc, ★ (2 dc, ch 2, 2 dc) in next corner ch-2 sp, dc in next 23 dc; repeat from ★ 2 times **more**, dc in same sp as first dc; join with slip st to first dc, finish off leaving a long end for sewing: 108 dc and 4 ch-2 sps.

12. Star

EASY +

Finished Size: 8" (20.5 cm) square

SHOPPING LIST

Yarn (Medium Weight) MEDIUM 4

- ☐ Blue - 36 yards (33 meters)
- ☐ Green - 18 yards (16.5 meters)
- ☐ Purple - 9 yards (8 meters)
- ☐ Brick Red - 7 yards (6.5 meters)

Crochet Hook

- ☐ Size I (5.5 mm) **or** size need for gauge

GAUGE INFORMATION

Rnds 1-4 = 4" (10 cm) square

STITCH GUIDE

TREBLE CROCHET

(abbreviated tr)

YO twice, insert hook in sc indicated, YO and pull up a loop (4 loops on hook), (YO and draw through 2 loops on hook) 3 times.

DOUBLE TREBLE CROCHET

(abbreviated dtr)

YO 3 times, insert hook in sc indicated, YO and pull up a loop (5 loops on hook), (YO and draw through 2 loops on hook) 4 times.

INSTRUCTIONS

With Green, ch 4; join with slip st to form a ring.

Rnd 1 (Right side)**:** Ch 1, ★ sc in ring, **[**ch 5, sc in second ch from hook and in next 3 chs **(spoke made)]**; repeat from ★ 4 times **more**; join with slip st to first sc, finish off: 5 sc and 5 spokes.

Note: Loop a short piece of yarn around any stitch to mark Rnd 1 as **right** side.

Rnd 2: With **right** side facing, join Purple with sc in skipped ch at tip of any spoke ***(see Joining With Sc, page 92)***; skip next 4 sc on same spoke, (dtr, 2 tr, dtr) in next sc **(between spokes)**, ★ sc in skipped ch at tip of next spoke, skip next 4 sc on same spoke, (dtr, 2 tr, dtr) in next sc **(between spokes)**; repeat from ★ 3 times **more**; join with slip st to first sc: 25 sts.

Rnd 3: Ch 1, sc in same st and in next dtr, 2 hdc in each of next 2 tr, (sc in next 3 sts, 2 hdc in each of next 2 tr) 4 times, 2 sc in last dtr; join with slip st to first sc, finish off: 36 sts.

Rnd 4: With **right** side facing, join Brick Red with dc in same st as joining ***(see Joining With Dc, page 92)***; (dc, ch 2, 2 dc) in same st, dc in next st, hdc in next 2 sts, sc in next 2 sts, hdc in next 2 sts, dc in next st, ★ (2 dc, ch 2, 2 dc) in next st, dc in next st, hdc in next 2 sts, sc in next 2 sts, hdc in next 2 sts, dc in next st; repeat from ★ 2 times **more**; join with slip st to first dc, finish off: 48 sts and 4 ch-2 sps.

Rnd 5: With **right** side facing, join Green with sc in any corner ch-2 sp; 2 sc in same sp, sc in next 12 sts, (3 sc in next corner ch-2 sp, sc in next 12 sts) around; join with slip st to first sc, finish off: 60 sc.

Rnd 6: With **right** side facing, join Blue with dc in center sc of any corner 3-sc group; dc in next 14 sc, ★ (dc, ch 2, dc) in next corner sc, dc in next 14 sc; repeat from ★ 2 times **more**, dc in same st as first dc, ch 1, sc in first dc to form last ch-2 sp: 64 dc and 4 ch-2 sps.

Rnd 7: Ch 3 (**counts as first dc, now and throughout**), dc in last ch-2 sp made, dc in next 16 dc, ★ (2 dc, ch 2, 2 dc) in next corner ch-2 sp, dc in next 16 dc; repeat from ★ 2 times **more**, 2 dc in same sp as first dc, ch 1, sc in first dc to form last ch-2 sp: 80 dc and 4 ch-2 sps.

Rnd 8: Ch 3, dc in last ch-2 sp made, dc in next 20 dc, ★ (2 dc, ch 2, 2 dc) in next corner ch-2 sp, dc in next 20 dc; repeat from ★ 2 times **more**, 2 dc in same sp as first dc, ch 2; join with slip st to first dc, finish off: 96 dc and 4 ch-2 sps.

Rnd 9: With **right** side facing, join Green with sc in any corner ch-2 sp; sc in same sp and in next 24 dc, (3 sc in next corner ch-2 sp, sc in next 24 dc) 3 times, sc in same sp as first sc; join with slip st to first sc, finish off leaving a long end for sewing: 108 sc.

BONUS SQUARES

13. Cabled Braids

INTERMEDIATE

Finished Size: 8" (20.5 cm) square

SHOPPING LIST

Yarn (Medium Weight) MEDIUM 4

- ☐ 83 yards (76 meters)

Crochet Hook

- ☐ Size I (5.5 mm) **or** size need for gauge

GAUGE INFORMATION

In pattern, 10 hdc = 3" (7.5 cm); 6 rows = 2" (5 cm)

STITCH GUIDE

FRONT POST TREBLE CROCHET *(abbreviated FPtr)*

YO twice, insert hook from **front** to **back** around post of st indicated 2 rows **below** *(Fig. 3, page 94)*, YO and pull up a loop (4 loops on hook), (YO and draw through 2 loops on hook) 3 times.

FRONT POST DOUBLE TREBLE CROCHET *(abbreviated FPdtr)*

YO 3 times, insert hook from **front** to **back** around post of st indicated 2 rows **below** *(Fig. 3, page 94)*, YO and pull up a loop (5 loops on hook), (YO and draw through 2 loops on hook) 4 times.

INSTRUCTIONS

Ch 27.

Row 1 (Right side)**:** Hdc in third ch from hook **(2 skipped chs count as first hdc)** and in each ch across: 26 hdc.

Note: Loop a short piece of yarn around any hdc to mark Row 1 as **right** side.

Row 2: Ch 2 **(counts as first hdc, now and throughout)**, turn; hdc in next hdc and in each hdc across.

Row 3: Ch 2, turn; hdc in next hdc, working post sts around hdc on Row 1, skip first 4 hdc, work FPdtr around each of next 2 hdc, working **behind** 2 FPdtr just made, work FPdtr around each of 2 hdc **before** FPdtr just made, work FPtr around each of next 2 hdc, skip 6 hdc **behind** post sts just made, hdc in next 2 hdc, ★ skip next 4 hdc from last hdc worked around, work FPdtr around each of next 2 hdc, working **behind** 2 FPdtr just made, work FPdtr around each of 2 hdc **before** FPdtr just made, work FPtr around each of next 2 hdc, skip 6 hdc **behind** post sts just made, hdc in next 2 hdc; repeat from ★ once **more**: 8 hdc and 18 post sts.

Row 4: Ch 2, turn; hdc in next hdc and in each st across.

Work all post stitches around post stitches 2 rows **below.**

Row 5: Ch 2, turn; hdc in next hdc, ★ work FPtr around each of next 2 FPdtr, skip next 2 FPdtr, work FPdtr around each of next 2 FPtr, working in **front** of 2 FPdtr just made, work FPdtr around each of 2 skipped FPdtr, skip 6 hdc **behind** post sts just made, hdc in next 2 hdc; repeat from ★ 2 times **more**.

Row 6: Ch 2, turn; hdc in next hdc and in each st across.

Row 7: Ch 2, turn; hdc in next hdc, ★ skip next 2 FPtr, work FPdtr around each of next 2 FPdtr, working **behind** 2 FPdtr just made, work FPdtr around each of 2 skipped FPtr, work FPtr around each of next 2 FPdtr, skip 6 hdc **behind** post sts just made, hdc in next 2 hdc; repeat from ★ 2 times **more**.

Row 8: Ch 2, turn; hdc in next hdc and in each st across.

Repeat Rows 5-8 for pattern until Square measures approximately 8" (20.5 cm) from beginning ch, ending by working a **wrong** side row.

Finish off, leaving a long end for sewing.

14. Cables 'n Ribs

INTERMEDIATE

Finished Size: 8" (20.5 cm) square

SHOPPING LIST

Yarn (Medium Weight) MEDIUM 4

☐ 82 yards (75 meters)

Crochet Hook

☐ Size I (5.5 mm)
or size need for gauge

GAUGE INFORMATION

In pattern, 10 hdc = 3" (7.5 cm);
6 rows = 2" (5 cm)

STITCH GUIDE

FRONT POST TREBLE CROCHET *(abbreviated FPtr)*

YO twice, insert hook from **front** to **back** around post of st indicated 2 rows **below** *(Fig. 3, page 94)*, YO and pull up a loop (4 loops on hook), (YO and draw through 2 loops on hook) 3 times.

FRONT POST DOUBLE TREBLE CROCHET *(abbreviated FPdtr)*

YO 3 times, insert hook from **front** to **back** around post of st indicated 2 rows **below** *(Fig. 3, page 94)*, YO and pull up a loop (5 loops on hook), (YO and draw through 2 loops on hook) 4 times.

INSTRUCTIONS

Ch 27.

Row 1 (Right side)**:** Hdc in third ch from hook **(2 skipped chs count as first hdc)** and in each ch across: 26 hdc.

Note: Loop a short piece of yarn around any hdc to mark Row 1 as **right** side.

Row 2: Ch 2 **(counts as first hdc, now and throughout)**, turn; hdc in next hdc and in each hdc across.

Row 3: Ch 2, turn; hdc in next hdc, working post sts around hdc on Row 1, skip first 4 hdc, work FPdtr around each of next 2 hdc, working in **front** of 2 FPdtr just made, work FPdtr around each of 2 hdc **before** FPdtr just made, skip 4 hdc **behind** post sts just made, hdc in next 2 hdc, ★ skip next 2 hdc from last hdc worked around, work FPtr around next hdc, skip hdc **behind** FPtr just made, hdc in next 2 hdc, skip next 4 hdc from last hdc worked around, work FPdtr around each of next 2 hdc, working in **front** of 2 FPdtr just made, work FPdtr around each of 2 hdc **before** FPdtr just made, skip 4 hdc **behind** post sts just made, hdc in next 2 hdc; repeat from ★ once **more**: 12 hdc and 14 posts sts.

Row 4: Ch 2, turn; hdc in next hdc and in each st across.

Work all post stitches around post stitches 2 rows **below**.

Row 5: Ch 2, turn; hdc in next hdc, work FPtr around each of next 4 FPdtr, skip 4 hdc **behind** post sts just made, hdc in next 2 hdc, ★ work FPtr around next FPtr, skip hdc **behind** FPtr just made, hdc in next 2 hdc, work FPtr around each of next 4 FPdtr, skip 4 hdc **behind** post sts just made, hdc in next 2 hdc; repeat from ★ once **more**.

Row 6: Ch 2, turn; hdc in next hdc and in each st across.

Row 7: Ch 2, turn; hdc in next hdc, skip next 2 FPtr, work FPdtr around each of next 2 FPtr, working in **front** of 2 FPdtr just made, work FPdtr around each of 2 skipped FPtr, skip 4 hdc **behind** post sts just made, hdc in next 2 hdc, ★ work FPtr around next FPtr, skip hdc **behind** FPtr just made, hdc in next 2 hdc, skip next 2 FPtr, work FPdtr around each of next 2 FPtr, working in **front** of 2 FPdtr just made, work FPdtr around each of 2 skipped FPtr, skip 4 hdc **behind** post sts just made, hdc in next 2 hdc; repeat from ★ once **more**.

Row 8: Ch 2, turn; hdc in next hdc and in each st across.

Repeat Rows 5-8 for pattern until Square measures approximately 8" (20.5 cm) from beginning ch, ending by working a **right** side row.

Finish off, leaving a long end for sewing.

15. Checkerboard

EASY

Finished Size: 8" (20.5 cm) square

SHOPPING LIST

Yarn (Medium Weight) MEDIUM 4

- ☐ Rust - 34 yards (31 meters)
- ☐ Gold - 34 yards (31 meters)

Crochet Hook

- ☐ Size I (5.5 mm) **or** size need for gauge

GAUGE INFORMATION

In pattern, 12 dc = 3¼" (8.25 cm);
4 rows = 2" (5 cm)

INSTRUCTIONS

With Rust, ch 32.

Row 1 (Right side)**:** Dc in fourth ch from hook **(3 skipped chs count as first dc)**, dc in next ch changing to Gold *(Figs. 2a & c, page 93)*, dc in next 3 chs changing to Rust in last dc made, ★ dc in next 3 chs changing to Gold in last dc made, dc in next 3 chs changing to Rust in last dc made; repeat from ★ across: 30 dc.

Note: Loop a short piece of yarn around any dc to mark Row 1 as **right** side.

Row 2: Ch 3 **(counts as first dc)**, turn; dc in next 2 dc changing to Gold in last dc made, dc in next 3 dc changing to Rust in last dc made, ★ dc in next 3 dc changing to Gold in last dc made, dc in next 3 dc changing to Rust in last dc made; repeat from ★ across.

Repeat Row 2 for pattern until Square measures approximately 8" (20.5 cm) from beginning ch, ending by working a **wrong** side row.

Finish off, leaving a long end for sewing.

16. Teardrops

EASY +

Finished Size: 8" (20.5 cm) square

Shown on page 65.

SHOPPING LIST

Yarn (Medium Weight) MEDIUM 4

- ☐ Rust - 30 yards (27.5 meters)
- ☐ Berry - 24 yards (22 meters)
- ☐ Gold - 24 yards (22 meters)

Crochet Hook

- ☐ Size I (5.5 mm) **or** size need for gauge

GAUGE INFORMATION

In pattern, 8 sts = 2¼" (5.75 cm); 8 rows = 2½" (6.25 cm)

STITCH GUIDE

TREBLE CROCHET *(abbreviated tr)*

YO twice, insert hook in st indicated, YO and pull up a loop (4 loops on hook), (YO and draw through 2 loops on hook) 3 times.

INSTRUCTIONS

With Rust, ch 30.

Row 1 (Right side)**:** Sc in second ch from hook and in next ch, ch 1, ★ skip next ch, sc in next 3 chs, ch 1; repeat from ★ across to last 3 chs, skip next ch, sc in last 2 chs: 22 sc and 7 ch-1 sps.

Note: Loop a short piece of yarn around any sc to mark Row 1 as **right** side.

Row 2: Ch 3 (**counts as first dc, now and throughout**), turn; dc in next sc, ch 1, ★ skip next ch-1 sp, dc in next 3 sc, ch 1; repeat from ★ across to last ch-1 sp, skip last ch-1 sp, dc in last 2 sc; finish off.

Work in the following color sequence: ★ 2 Rows **each** of Berry, Gold, Rust; repeat from ★ for color sequence.

Row 3: With **right** side facing, join next color with sc in first dc *(see Joining With Sc, page 92)*; sc in next dc, working **around** previous 2 rows *(Fig. 4, page 94)*, tr in first skipped ch on beginning ch, ★ sc in next dc, ch 1, skip next dc, sc in next dc, working **around** previous 2 rows, tr in next skipped ch on beginning ch; repeat from ★ across to last 2 dc, sc in last 2 dc: 23 sts and 6 ch-1 sps.

Row 4: Ch 3, turn; dc in next 3 sts, ch 1, ★ skip next ch-1 sp, dc in next 3 sts, ch 1; repeat from ★ across to last ch-1 sp, skip last ch-1 sp, dc in last 4 sts; finish off.

Row 5: With **right** side facing, join next color with sc in first dc; sc in next dc, ch 1, ★ skip next dc, sc in next dc, working **around** previous 2 rows, tr in next skipped dc 3 rows **below**, sc in next dc, ch 1; repeat from ★ across to last 3 dc, skip next dc, sc in last 2 dc: 22 sts and 7 ch-1 sps.

Row 6: Ch 3, turn; dc in next sc, ch 1, ★ skip next ch-1 sp, dc in next 3 sts, ch 1; repeat from ★ across to last ch-1 sp, skip last ch-1 sp, dc in last 2 sc; finish off.

Row 7: With **right** side facing, join next color with sc in first dc; sc in next dc, working **around** previous 2 rows, tr in next skipped dc 3 rows **below**, ★ sc

in next dc, ch 1, skip next dc, sc in next dc, working **around** previous 2 rows, tr in next skipped dc 3 rows **below**; repeat from ★ across to last 2 dc, sc in last 2 dc: 23 sts and 6 ch-1 sps.

Rows 8-24: Repeat Rows 4-7, 4 times; then repeat Row 4 once **more**.

Row 25: With **right** side facing, join Rust with sc in first dc; ★ sc in next 3 dc, working **around** previous 2 rows, tr in next skipped dc 3 rows **below**; repeat from ★ across to last 4 dc, sc in last 4 dc: 29 sts.

Row 26: Ch 3, turn; dc in next sc and in each st across; finish off leaving a long end for sewing.

17. Textured Vees

EASY +

Finished Size: 8" (20.5 cm) square

SHOPPING LIST

Yarn (Medium Weight) MEDIUM 4

- ☐ Rust - 64 yards (58.5 meters)
- ☐ Dk Green - 17 yards (15.5 meters)
- ☐ Lt Green - 12 yards (11 meters)

Crochet Hook

- ☐ Size I (5.5 mm) **or** size need for gauge

Additional Supplies

- ☐ Safety pin

GAUGE INFORMATION

In pattern, 12 sc = 3½" (9 cm);
8 rows = 2¼" (5.75 cm)

INSTRUCTIONS

With Rust, ch 29.

Row 1: Dc in fourth ch from hook **(3 skipped chs count as first dc)** and in each ch across: 27 dc.

Row 2 (Right side)**:** Ch 1, turn; sc in each dc across.

Note: Loop a short piece of yarn around any sc to mark Row 2 as **right** side.

Row 3: Ch 1, turn; sc in each sc across; place loop from hook onto safety pin to keep piece from unraveling while working next row.

Row 4: With **right** side facing, join Dk Green with sc in first sc *(see Joining With Sc, page 92)*; sc in next 2 sc, **[**ch 4, skip first 3 dc on Row 1, sc around post of next dc, ch 4, skip next sc on Row 3 **(Vee made)]**, sc in next 3 sc, ★ ch 4, skip next 3 dc from last dc worked around, sc around post of next dc, ch 4, skip next sc on Row 3, sc in next 3 sc; repeat from ★ across; finish off: 21 sc and 6 Vees.

Row 5: With **right** side facing, place loop from safety pin onto hook; slip st in first sc, ch 3 **(counts as first dc, now and throughout)**, dc in next 2 sc, (dc in next Rust sc and in next 3 Dk Green sc) across: 27 dc.

Row 6: Ch 1, turn; sc in each dc across.

Row 7: Ch 1, turn; sc in each sc across; place loop from hook onto safety pin.

Row 8: With **right** side facing, join Lt Green with sc in first sc; sc in next 4 sc, ch 4, sc around post of next dc 3 rows **below** (center dc between Vees), ch 4, ★ skip next sc on previous row, sc in next 3 sc, ch 4, sc around post of next dc 3 rows **below**, ch 4; repeat from ★ across to last 6 sc on previous row, skip next sc, sc in last 5 sc; finish off: 22 sc and 5 Vees.

Row 9: With **wrong** side facing, place loop from safety pin onto hook; slip st in first sc, ch 3, dc in next 4 sc, dc in next Rust sc, (dc in next 3 Lt Green sc, dc in next Rust sc) across to last 5 Lt Green sc, dc in last 5 sc: 27 dc.

Row 10: Ch 1, turn; sc in each dc across.

Row 11: Ch 1, turn; sc in each sc across; place loop from hook onto safety pin.

Row 12: With **right** side facing, join Dk Green with sc in first sc; sc in next 2 sc, ★ ch 4, sc around post of next dc 3 rows **below**, ch 4, skip next sc on previous row, sc in next 3 sc; repeat from ★ across; finish off: 21 sc and 6 Vees.

Rows 13-29: Repeat Rows 5-12, 2 times; then repeat Row 5 once **more**.

Finish off, leaving a long end for sewing.

18. Wavy

EASY +

Finished Size: 8" (20.5 cm) square

SHOPPING LIST

Yarn (Medium Weight) MEDIUM 4

- ☐ Dk Green - 29 yards (26.5 meters)
- ☐ Gold - 23 yards (21 meters)
- ☐ Lt Green - 18 yards (16.5 meters)

Crochet Hook

- ☐ Size I (5.5 mm) **or** size need for gauge

GAUGE INFORMATION

In pattern, 6 sts = 2" (5 cm);
6 rows = 2½" (6.25 cm)

STITCH GUIDE

TREBLE CROCHET

(abbreviated tr)

YO twice, insert hook in sc indicated, YO and pull up a loop (4 loops on hook), (YO and draw through 2 loops on hook) 3 times.

SINGLE CROCHET 2 TOGETHER

(abbreviated sc2tog)

Pull up a loop in each of next 2 sts, YO and draw through all 3 loops on hook (**counts as one sc**).

SINGLE CROCHET 3 TOGETHER

(abbreviated sc3tog)

Pull up a loop in each of next 3 sts, YO and draw through all 4 loops on hook (**counts as one sc**).

TREBLE CROCHET 2 TOGETHER

(abbreviated tr2tog)

(uses next 2 sts)

★ YO twice, insert hook in **next** st, YO and pull up a loop, (YO and draw through 2 loops on hook) twice; repeat from ★ once **more**, YO and draw through all 3 loops on hook (**counts as one tr**).

TREBLE CROCHET 3 TOGETHER

(abbreviated tr3tog)

(uses next 3 sts)

★ YO twice, insert hook in **next** st, YO and pull up a loop, (YO and draw through 2 loops on hook) twice; repeat from ★ 2 times **more**, YO and draw through all 4 loops on hook (**counts as one tr**).

INSTRUCTIONS

With Dk Green, ch 26.

Row 1 (Right side): Sc in second ch from hook and in each ch across: 25 sc.

Note: Loop a short piece of yarn around any sc to mark Row 1 as **right** side.

Rows 2 and 3: Ch 1, turn; sc in each sc across.

Row 4: Ch 1, turn; sc in first sc, ★ hdc in next sc, dc in next sc, 3 tr in next sc, dc in next sc, hdc in next sc, sc in next sc; repeat from ★ across; finish off: 33 sts.

Row 5: With **right** side facing, join Lt Green with slip st in first sc; ch 1, beginning in same st, work sc2tog, sc in next 2 sts, 3 sc in next tr, sc in next 2 sts, ★ work sc3tog, sc in next 2 sts, 3 sc in next tr, sc in next 2 sts; repeat from ★ across to last 2 sts, work sc2tog.

Row 6: Ch 1, turn; beginning in first st, work sc2tog, sc in next 2 sc, 3 sc in next sc, sc in next 2 sc, ★ work sc3tog, sc in next 2 sc, 3 sc in next sc, sc in next 2 sc; repeat from ★ across to last 2 sc, work sc2tog; finish off.

Row 7: With **right** side facing, join Gold with slip st in first sc; ch 3, tr in next sc, dc in next sc, hdc in next sc, sc in next sc, hdc in next sc, dc in next sc, ★ work tr3tog, dc in next sc, hdc in next sc, sc in next sc, hdc in next sc, dc in next sc; repeat from ★ across to last 2 sts, work tr2tog: 25 sts.

Row 8: Ch 1, turn; sc in each st across to turning ch, leave turning ch unworked; finish off.

Row 9: With **right** side facing, join Dk Green with sc in first sc *(see Joining With Sc, page 92)*; sc in next sc and in each sc across.

Repeat Rows 4-9 for pattern until Square measures 8" (20.5 cm) from beginning ch, ending by working a sc row.

Finish off, leaving a long end for sewing.

19. Polka Dots

EASY +

Finished Size: 8" (20.5 cm) square

Shown on page 77.

SHOPPING LIST

Yarn (Medium Weight) MEDIUM 4

- ☐ Lt Green - 58 yards (53 meters)
- ☐ Dk Green - 45 yards (41 meters)

Crochet Hook

- ☐ Size I (5.5 mm) **or** size need for gauge

GAUGE INFORMATION

In pattern,

6 sc and 8 rows = 2" (5 cm)

STITCH GUIDE

TREBLE CROCHET *(abbreviated tr)*

YO twice, insert hook in sc indicated, YO and pull up a loop (4 loops on hook), (YO and draw through 2 loops on hook) 3 times.

DOUBLE TREBLE CROCHET *(abbreviated dtr)*

YO 3 times, insert hook in sc indicated, YO and pull up a loop (5 loops on hook), (YO and draw through 2 loops on hook) 4 times.

POLKA DOT (uses one sc)

(Dc, tr, dtr) in next sc changing to Lt Green in dtr *(Fig. 2a, page 93)*. Do **not** cut old color unless indicated. When working **next** row, work over carried strand *(Fig. 2c, page 93)*. Push Polka Dot to **right** side when working the next st.

INSTRUCTIONS

With Lt Green, ch 25.

Row 1 (Right side)**:** Sc in second ch from hook and in each ch across: 24 sc.

Note: Loop a short piece of yarn around any hdc to mark Row 1 as **right** side.

Row 2: Ch 1, turn; sc in first sc changing to Dk Green ***(Figs. 2a & c, page 93)***, work Polka Dot changing to Lt Green in last sc made, ★ sc in next 2 sc changing to Dk Green in last sc made, work Polka Dot changing to Lt Green; repeat from ★ across to last sc, cut Dk Green, sc in last sc: 16 sc and 8 Polka Dots.

Row 3: Ch 1, turn; sc in first sc, sc in dc of next Polka Dot, (sc in next 2 sc, sc in dc of next Polka Dot) across to last sc, sc in last sc: 24 sc.

Rows 4 and 5: Ch 1, turn; sc in each sc across.

Repeat Rows 2-5 for pattern until Square measures approximately 8" (20.5 cm) from beginning ch, ending by working Row 3.

Finish off, leaving a long end for sewing.

20. Snowflake

EASY +

Finished Size: 8" (20.5 cm) square

SHOPPING LIST

Yarn (Medium Weight) MEDIUM 4

- ☐ Dk Green - 58 yards (53 meters)
- ☐ Berry - 19 yards (17.5 meters)

Crochet Hook

- ☐ Size I (5.5 mm) **or** size need for gauge

GAUGE INFORMATION

In color pattern,

7 dc and 4 rows = 2" (5 cm)

INSTRUCTIONS

With Dk Green, ch 29.

Row 1 (Wrong side)**:** Sc in second ch from hook and in each ch across: 28 sc.

Note: Loop a short piece of yarn around the **back** of any sc on Row 1 to mark **right** side.

Rows 2-16: Ch 3 **(counts as first dc)**, turn; dc in next st and in each st across following chart ***(Figs. 2a & c, page 93)***.

Row 17: Ch 1, turn; sc in each dc across.

Cut Berry and finish off Dk Green, leaving a long end for sewing.

KEY

Berry

Dk Green

CHART

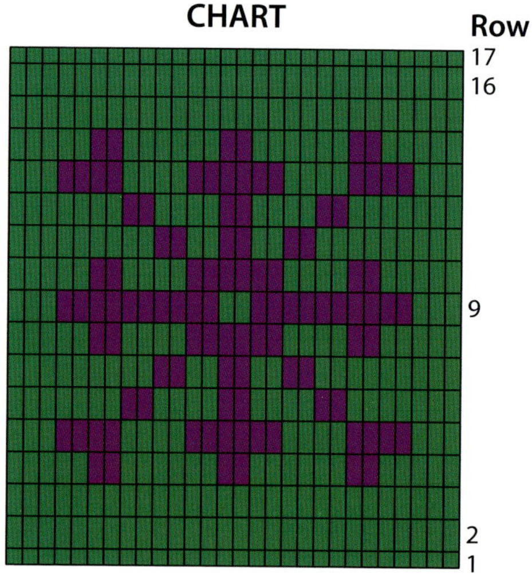

Note: On Rows 1 and 17, each square on chart represents one single crochet; on Rows 2-16, each rectangle represents one double crochet.

21. Mitered Square

EASY +

Finished Size: 8" (20.5 cm) square *Shown on page 83.*

SHOPPING LIST

Yarn (Medium Weight) MEDIUM 4

- ☐ Rust - 30 yards (27.5 meters)
- ☐ Dk Green - 20 yards (18.5 meters)
- ☐ Lt Green - 15 yards (13.5 meters)

Crochet Hook

- ☐ Size I (5.5 mm) **or** size need for gauge

GAUGE INFORMATION

7 dc and 4 rows = 2" (5 cm)

Rows 1-5 = 2¾" (7 cm) square

INSTRUCTIONS

Row 1 (Right side)**:** With Rust, ch 2, 3 sc in second ch from hook.

Note: Loop a short piece of yarn around any sc to mark Row 1 as **right** side.

Row 2: Ch 3 **(counts as first dc, now and throughout)**, turn; (dc, ch 2, dc) in next sc, dc in last sc: 4 dc and one ch-2 sp.

Row 3: Ch 3, turn; dc in next dc, (2 dc, ch 2, 2 dc) in next ch-2 sp, dc in last 2 dc; finish off: 8 dc and one ch-2 sp.

Row 4: With **wrong** side facing, join Lt Green with dc in first dc *(see Joining With Dc, page 92)*; dc in next dc and in each dc across to next ch-2 sp, (2 dc, ch 2, 2 dc) in ch-2 sp, dc in each dc across: 12 dc and one ch-2 sp.

Row 5: Ch 3, turn; dc in next dc and in each dc across to next ch-2 sp, (2 dc, ch 2, 2 dc) in ch-2 sp, dc in each dc across; finish off: 16 dc and one ch-2 sp.

Rows 6-15: Repeat Rows 4 and 5, 5 times, working in the following color sequence: 2 Rows **each** of Dk Green, Rust, Lt Green, Dk Green, Rust: 56 dc and one ch-2 sp.

Finish off, leaving a long end for sewing.

22. Cross Stitch Stripes

EASY

Finished Size: 8" (20.5 cm) square

SHOPPING LIST

Yarn (Medium Weight) MEDIUM 4

- ☐ Gold - 30 yards (27.5 meters)
- ☐ Rust - 17 yards (15.5 meters)
- ☐ Dk Green - 17 yards (15.5 meters)

Crochet Hook

- ☐ Size I (5.5 mm) **or** size need for gauge

GAUGE INFORMATION

In pattern, 10 sc = 3" (7.5 cm); 6 rows = 2" (5 cm)

— STITCH GUIDE —

TREBLE CROCHET *(abbreviated tr)*

YO twice, insert hook in sc indicated, YO and pull up a loop (4 loops on hook), (YO and draw through 2 loops on hook) 3 times.

INSTRUCTIONS

With Gold, ch 27.

Row 1 (Right side)**:** Sc in second ch from hook and in each ch across: 26 sc.

Note: Loop a short piece of yarn around any sc to mark Row 1 as **right** side.

Row 2: Ch 1, turn; sc in each sc across; finish off.

Row 3: With **right** side facing, join Dk Green with sc in first sc *(see Joining With Sc, page 92)*; sc in next sc and in each sc across.

Row 4: Ch 3 **(counts as first dc)**, turn; ★ skip next 2 sc, tr in next sc, ch 1, working in **front** of tr just made *(Fig. 5, page 94)*, tr in first skipped sc **(Cross St made)**; repeat from ★ across to last sc, dc in last sc: 8 Cross Sts.

Row 5: Ch 1, turn; sc in each st and in each ch-1 sp across; finish off: 26 sc.

Row 6: With **right** side facing, join Gold with sc in first sc; sc in next sc and in each sc across.

Rows 7 and 8: Ch 1, turn; sc in each sc across; at end of Row 8, finish off.

Rows 9-11: With Rust, repeat Rows 3-5.

Rows 12-14: Repeat Rows 6-8.

Rows 15-23: Repeat Rows 3-11.

Row 24: With **right** side facing, join Gold with sc in first sc; sc in next sc and in each sc across.

Row 25: Ch 1, turn; sc in each sc across; finish off leaving a long end for sewing.

THROW

EASY +

Finished Size: 48½" x 64½" (123 cm x 164 cm) *Shown on page 89.*

SHOPPING LIST

Yarn (Medium Weight) MEDIUM 4

- ☐ Gold - 1,180 yards (1,079 meters)
- ☐ Rust - 985 yards (901 meters)
- ☐ Dk Green - 985 yards (901 meters
- ☐ Berry - 395 yards (361 meters)
- ☐ Lt Green - 395 yards (361 meters)

Crochet Hook

- ☐ Size I (5.5 mm) **or** size needed for gauge

Additional Supplies

- ☐ Yarn needle

GAUGE INFORMATION

Each Square = 8" (20.5 cm)

INSTRUCTIONS

Squares

Make a total of 48 Squares.

Make 4 **each**:

1. Daisy, page 4.

3. Zinnia, page 12.

13. Cabled Braids, page 52.

14. Cables 'N Ribs, page 56.

16. Teardrops, page 63.

17. Textured Vees, page 66.

18. Wavy, page 70.

21. Mitered Square, page 81.

22. Cross Stitch Stripes, page 84.

Make 3 **each**:

2. Concentric Circles, page 8.
15. Checkerboard, page 60.
19. Polka Dots, page 75.
20. Snowflake, page 78.

Block each Square to measure 8" (20.5 cm) *(see Blocking, page 94)*.

Assembly

With **wrong** sides together and using Placement Diagram as a guide, whipstitch Squares together *(Figs. 6a & b, page 95)*, forming 6 vertical strips of 8 Squares each, beginning and ending in corners; then whipstitch strips together in same manner.

Edging

Rnd 1: With **right** side facing, join Gold with sc in any st; sc evenly around working 3 sc in each corner; join with slip st to first sc.

Rnd 2: Ch 1, do **not** turn; working from **left** to **right**, work reverse sc in each sc around *(Figs. 1a-d, page 92)*; join with slip st to first st, finish off.

PLACEMENT DIAGRAM

13	16	1	22	3	18
15	20	14	2	19	17
18	3	22	1	16	13
17	14	*21	*21	20	15
19	2	*21	*21	17	14
13	16	1	22	3	18
17	19	2	14	20	15
18	3	22	1	16	13

* As you assemble strips, turn the four Mitered Squares to form a large square.

GENERAL INSTRUCTIONS

ABBREVIATIONS

ch(s)	chain(s)
cm	centimeters
dc	double crochet(s)
dtr	double treble crochet(s)
FPdtr	Front Post double treble crochet(s)
FPtr	Front Post treble crochet(s)
hdc	half double crochet(s)
mm	millimeters
Rnd(s)	Round(s)
sc2tog	single crochet 2 together
sc3tog	single crochet 3 together
sc	single crochet(s)
sp(s)	space(s)
st(s)	stitch(es)
tr2tog	treble crochet 2 together
tr3tog	treble crochet 3 together
tr	treble crochet(s)
YO	yarn over

SYMBOLS & TERMS

★ — work instructions following ★ as many **more** times as indicated in addition to the first time.

† to † — work all instructions from first † to second † **as many** times as specified.

( ) or **[ ]** — work enclosed instructions **as many** times as specified by the number immediately following **or** work all enclosed instructions in the stitch or space indicated **or** contains explanatory remarks.

colon (:) — the numbers given after a colon at the end of a row or round denotes the number of stitches or spaces you should have on that row or round.

CROCHET TERMINOLOGY		
UNITED STATES		INTERNATIONAL
slip stitch (slip st)	=	single crochet (sc)
single crochet (sc)	=	double crochet (dc)
half double crochet (hdc)	=	half treble crochet (htr)
double crochet (dc)	=	treble crochet (tr)
treble crochet (tr)	=	double treble crochet (dtr)
double treble crochet (dtr)	=	triple treble crochet (ttr)
triple treble crochet (tr tr)	=	quadruple treble crochet (qtr)
skip	=	miss

GAUGE

Exact gauge is **essential** for proper size. Before beginning your project, make a sample swatch in the yarn and hook specified in the individual instructions. After completing the swatch, measure it, counting your stitches and rows or rounds carefully. If your swatch is larger or smaller than specified, **make another, changing hook size to get the correct gauge**. Keep trying until you find the size hook that will give you the specified gauge.

CROCHET HOOKS																	
U.S.	B-1	C-2	D-3	E-4	F-5	G-6	7	H-8	I-9	J-10	K-10½	L-11	M/N-13	N/P-15	P/Q	Q	S
Metric - mm	2.25	2.75	3.25	3.5	3.75	4	4.5	5	5.5	6	6.5	8	9	10	15	16	19

BEGINNER	Projects for first-time crocheters using basic stitches. Minimal shaping.
EASY	Projects using yarn with basic stitches, repetitive stitch patterns, simple color changes, and simple shaping and finishing.
INTERMEDIATE	Projects using a variety of techniques, such as basic lace patterns or color patterns, mid-level shaping and finishing.
EXPERIENCED	Projects with intricate stitch patterns, techniques and dimension, such as non-repeating patterns, multi-color techniques, fine threads, small hooks, detailed shaping and refined finishing.

Yarn Weight Symbol & Names	LACE 0	SUPER FINE 1	FINE 2	LIGHT 3	MEDIUM 4	BULKY 5	SUPER BULKY 6	JUMBO 7
Type of Yarns in Category	Fingering, size 10 crochet thread	Sock, Fingering, Baby	Sport, Baby	DK, Light Worsted	Worsted, Afghan, Aran	Chunky, Craft, Rug	Super Bulky, Roving	Jumbo, Roving
Crochet Gauge* Ranges in Single Crochet to 4" (10 cm)	32-42 sts**	21-32 sts	16-20 sts	12-17 sts	11-14 sts	8-11 sts	6-9 sts	5 sts and fewer
Advised Hook Size Range	Steel*** 6 to 8, Regular hook B-1	B-1 to E-4	E-4 to 7	7 to I-9	I-9 to K-10½	K-10½ to M/N-13	M/N-13 to Q	Q and larger

*GUIDELINES ONLY: The chart above reflects the most commonly used gauges and hook sizes for specific yarn categories.

** Lace weight yarns are usually crocheted with larger hooks to create lacy openwork patterns. Accordingly, a gauge range is difficult to determine. Always follow the gauge stated in your pattern.

*** Steel crochet hooks are sized differently from regular hooks–the higher the number, the smaller the hook, which is the reverse of regular hook sizing.

JOINING WITH SC

When instructed to join with sc, begin with a slip knot on hook. Insert hook in stitch or space indicated, YO and pull up a loop, YO and draw through both loops on hook.

JOINING WITH DC

When instructed to join with dc, begin with a slip knot on hook. YO, holding loop on hook, insert hook in stitch or space indicated, YO and pull up a loop (3 loops on hook), (YO and draw through 2 loops on hook) twice.

REVERSE SINGLE CROCHET

(abbreviated reverse sc)

Working from **left** to **right**, ★ insert hook in sc to right of hook *(Fig. 1a)*, YO and draw through, under and to left of loop on hook (2 loops on hook) *(Fig. 1b)*, YO and draw through both loops on hook *(Fig. 1c)* (reverse sc made, *Fig. 1d)*; repeat from ★ around.

Fig. 1a

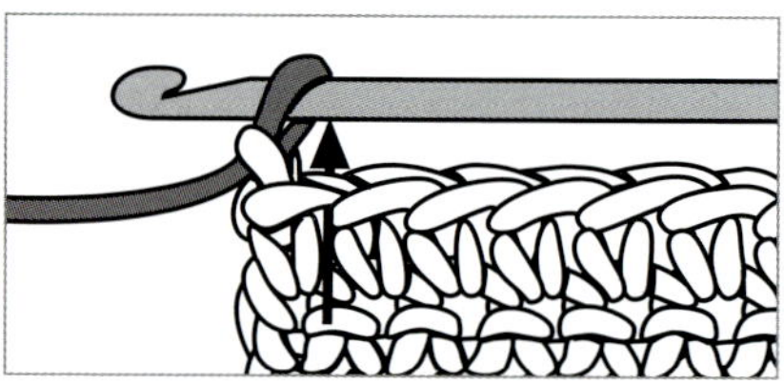

Fig. 1b

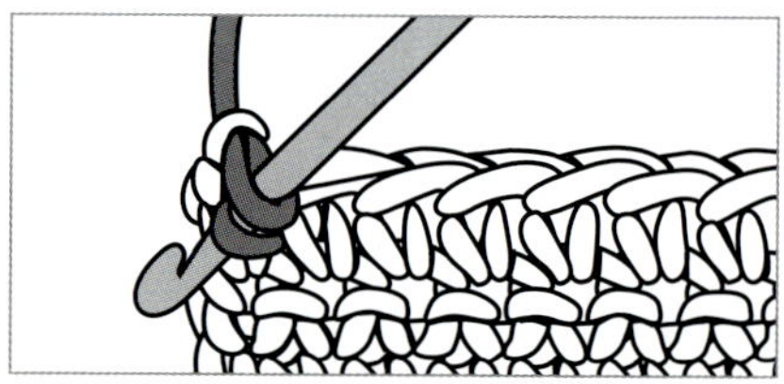

Fig. 1c

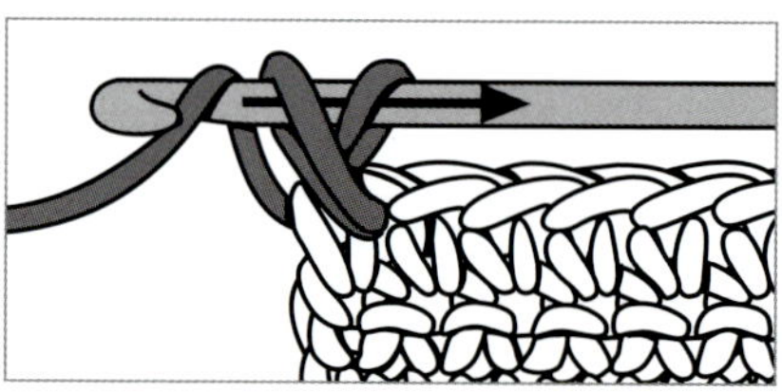

Fig. 1d

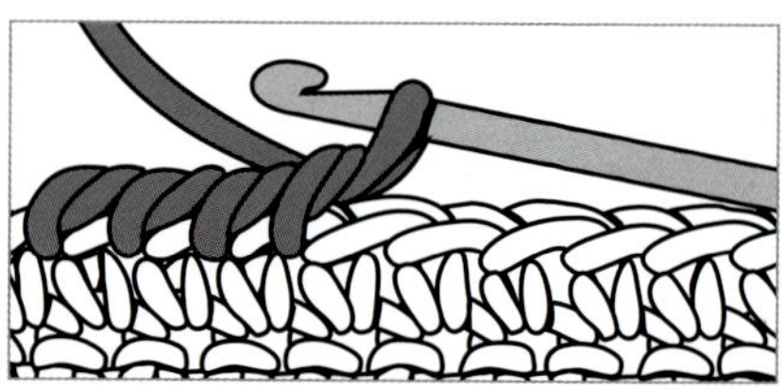

CHANGING COLORS

Work the last stitch to within one step of completion, drop yarn to **wrong** side, hook new yarn *(Figs. 2a & b)* and draw through all loops on hook.

When using two colors across one row, carry unused color loosely across **wrong** side of work. When working **next** row, work over carried strand *(Fig. 2c)*. Cut yarns when they are no longer needed.

Fig. 2a

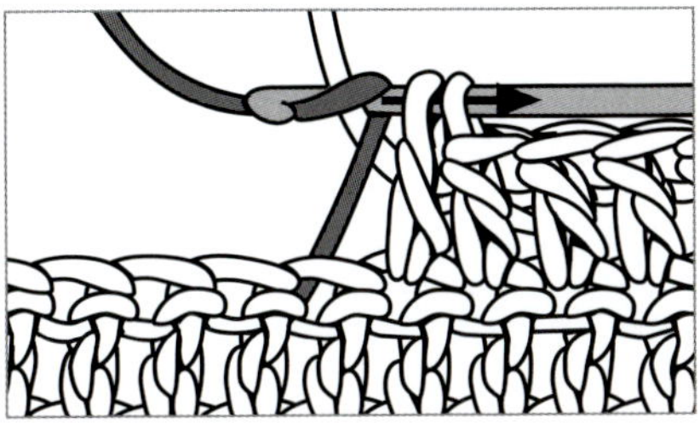

Fig. 2b

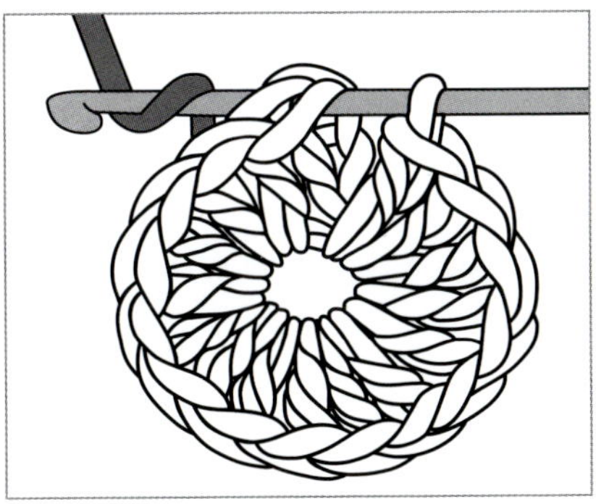

Fig. 2c

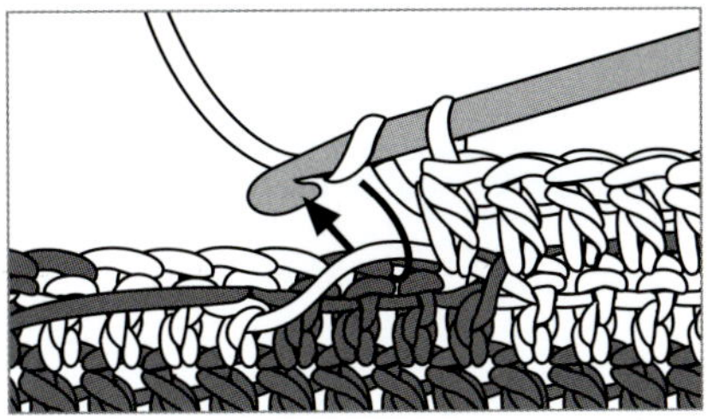

POST STITCH

Work around post of stitch indicated, inserting hook in direction of arrow *(Fig. 3)*.

Fig. 3

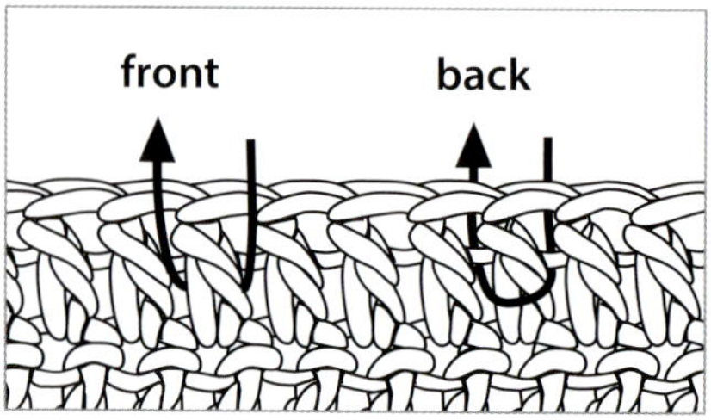

WORKING AROUND A STITCH

Work in stitch or space indicated, inserting hook in direction of arrow *(Fig. 4)*.

Fig. 4

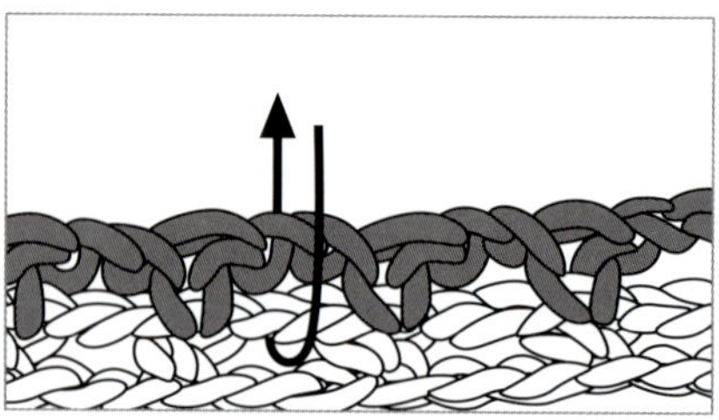

WORKING IN FRONT OF A STITCH

Work in stitch or space indicated, inserting hook in direction of arrow *(Fig. 5)*.

Fig. 5

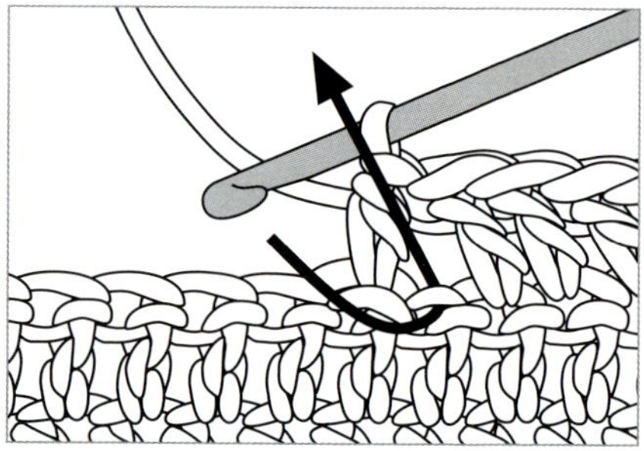

BLOCKING

Follow the instructions on the yarn label or block as follows: For wool, steam the Square supporting the weight of the iron at all times. Allow the Square to dry flat, away from heat or sunlight.

For synthetic and blends, submerge the Square in cool water. Roll the Square in a clean terry towel and gently press out the excess moisture. Lay the Square flat and allow to dry completely, away from heat and sunlight.

WHIPSTITCH

Place two Squares with **wrong** sides together. Beginning in center of corner, sew through both pieces once to secure the beginning of the seam, leaving an ample yarn end to weave in later. Insert the needle from **back** to **front** through both loops *(Fig. 6a)* **or** in end of rows *(Fig. 6b)* on both Squares. Bring the needle around and insert it from **back** to **front** through next loops on both Squares. Continue in this manner across to corner, keeping the sewing yarn fairly loose.

Fig. 6a

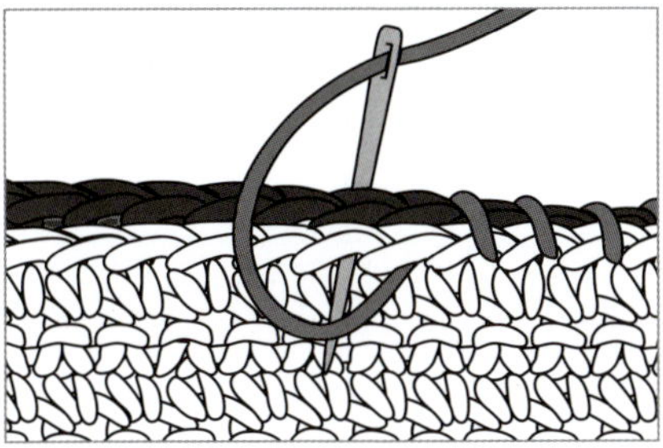

Fig. 6b

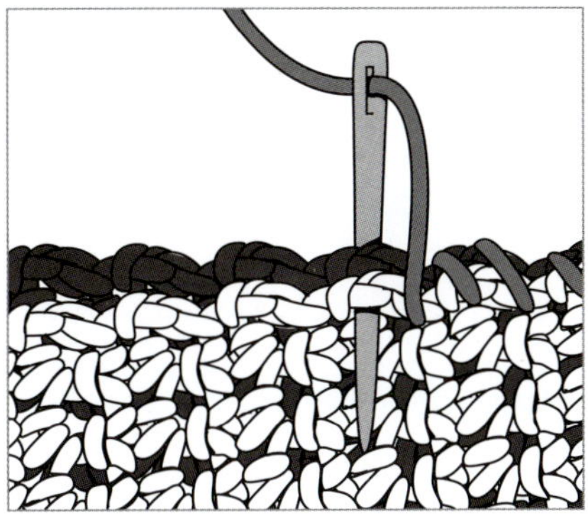

YARN INFORMATION

The Throw and Squares in this book were made using Medium Weight Yarn. Any brand of Medium Weight Yarn may be used. It is best to refer to the yardage/meters when determining how many balls or skeins to purchase. Remember, to arrive at the finished size, it is the GAUGE/ TENSION that is important, not the brand of yarn.

For your convenience, listed below are specific yarns used to create our photography models. Because yarn manufacturers make frequent changes in their product lines, you may sometimes find it necessary to use a substitute yarn or to search for the discontinued product at alternate suppliers (locally or online).

Lion Brand® Wool-Ease®
Gold - #171 Gold
Rust - #188 Paprika
Dk Green - #172 Avocado
Berry - #196 Zinnia
Lt Green - #172 Lemongrass

Lion Brand® Vanna's Choice®
Purple - #147 Purple
Red - #133 Brick

Red Heart® With Love®
Lt Blue - #1502 Iced Aqua
Blue - #1623 Mallard

Bernat® Super Value™
Green - #53222 Fern